Major League Soccer

SOCCER

Atlanta United FC

John Bankston

Printing   1   2   3   4   5   6   7   8

First Edition, 2020.
Author: John Bankston
Designer: Ed Morgan
Editor: Lisa Petrillo

Series: Major League Soccer
Title: Atlanta United / by John Bankston

Hallandale, FL : Mitchell Lane Publishers, [2020]

Library bound ISBN: 9781680204766
eBook ISBN: 9781680204773

PHOTO CREDITS: Design Elements, freepik.com, p.12 Thomson200 Public Domain, AP Images

Contents

Words in **bold** throughout
can be found in the Glossary.

Georgia Pride

Georgia has a lot to offer. More movies and TV shows are filmed there than anywhere in the U.S., other than New York or California. Nearly six million people live in and around Atlanta, its largest city. Major companies like CNN, Coca-Cola, and UPS are based there. In 2017, it would finally have a Major League Soccer team.

Just like football, baseball, and basketball, soccer has a major league. Major leagues attract the best athletes. Their players earn the most money. The teams draw the most fans.

Across the world, soccer is more popular than other sports. It is often called "football." Southern states like Georgia are better known for American football. College teams like the University of Georgia Bulldogs and pro teams like the Atlanta Falcons play to packed **stadiums**. Some believed soccer would not be as popular in Atlanta. In 2017, the sport's fans proved them wrong.

Soccer in Georgia was first played by **immigrants**. John H. Harland played the sport in Northern Ireland. After **emigrating** to the U.S. in 1906, he continued playing. Harland loved it so much, he started a league using mostly immigrant workers from his printing company.

Soccer faced challenges. When Emory University in Atlanta began its program in 1958, the team had to travel out of state. There weren't enough teams to play against in Georgia.

Professional soccer did not do much better. In 1967, the Atlanta Chiefs began playing in the North American Soccer League. The next year they beat top-rated Manchester City of the English First Division. More than 23,000 fans showed up to watch, as one reporter described it, "England suffered her worst defeat on American soil since the War of 1812 Monday night at Atlanta Stadium." They went on to be League champions that year. Despite the great start, the team folded in 1972. In 1979, billionaire investor Ted Turner bought a new version of the team. Turner, the owner of CNN, couldn't save the Chiefs, who folded for the second time in 1981.

After that, Georgia soccer fans worried the sport would never succeed in their state. Two major events changed soccer's future.

In 1996, Atlanta hosted the Olympic Games. Soccer teams from countries across the world competed in five American cities. The winners in Birmingham, Alabama, Miami and Orlando, Florida, and Washington, D.C., traveled to the final round at Sanford Stadium in Athens, Georgia. The U.S. women's team reached the finals. The men's did not. On August 1, 1996, more than 76,000 people watched the U.S. team beat China 2–1. The women had won the gold!

Fans hold up a sign during a USA versus China Women's Soccer match at the Atlanta Olympic Games in 1996.

Major League Soccer's first season was also in 1996. The League was born because of the World Cup.

The World Cup is soccer's most important **tournament**. Every four years, a different country hosts 32 different teams. The U.S. wanted to be a host. To become a host, the country first needed a top-level pro league.

When the U.S. hosted the 1994 World Cup, it broke records for attendance. At every match, 70,000 people filled the stands. No World Cup has ever attracted so many people. It was a good sign for Major League Soccer.

MLS began with just 10 teams. Most played to half-empty stands. The Miami and Tampa teams folded in 2001. In 2004, the League lost $350 million. Lots of people thought MLS would soon disappear.

The World Cup gave MLS its start. It also kept it alive. In 2002, the U.S. reached the Cup's quarterfinals. People who had never watched soccer before tuned in to cheer for the U.S. team. Afterward, they started following MLS teams. By the 2010s, the League had expanded and attendance grew.

In 2018, the U.S. team did not qualify for the World Cup. The nation's soccer fans still watched. Many cheered on countries from where their families had emigrated. When France reached the Final, Atlanta's French-American Chamber of Commerce chapter organized a World Cup party. Fans from the Consulate General France, Francophonie Atlanta, and the Alliance Française got to enjoy France's victory over Croatia 4–2. The last time the country won was in 1998.

Today MLS has grown to 23 teams in the U.S. and Canada. There will be new teams in Cincinnati, Ohio, in 2019, while Miami and Nashville, Tennessee, will field new teams in 2020.

Teams compete in two divisions, the Eastern and Western. Clubs play 17 home games, and 17 away.

The season is March to October. Points determine the playoffs. Wins earn teams three points. Ties earn one point. Losses get no points. When the season ends, the 12 teams with the most points enter the playoffs. Six teams are from the Western Conference, and six from the Eastern Conference. The MLS Championship is decided in December.

Atlanta's MLS team would have to wait until 2017 to compete for the championship. Two years before, fans learned their team would be called "Atlanta United FC."

In Georgia more than 100,000 people play soccer. That's twice as many as were playing when MLS began.

On July 7, 2015, nearly 5,000 fans gathered in Atlanta to celebrate the club's naming. Darren Eales told *Georgia Trend* magazine, "It was good fun, good energy, and great singing. That's the type of thing that we hope Atlanta United gets known for."

For Major League Soccer, 2015 was a very good year. The League broke attendance records. The average game attracted more than 21,000 fans. There were more people watching than the premiere leagues of Brazil, France, and Argentina, among others. Still, would MLS catch on in Atlanta?

Fun Facts

1 There have been more than one dozen pro men's and women's soccer teams in Georgia over the last 50 years.

2 The Atlanta Silverbacks played in North American Soccer League from 2010 to 2015. Today the team is in the National Premier Soccer League along with the Georgia Revolution.

Great Beginnings

CHAPTER TWO

Atlanta United FC had been playing for just 25 minutes when Yamil Asad scored the team's first goal. The stadium was packed. The crowd roared.

It was the first Sunday in March. Any doubts about the city's love for soccer had been erased. More than 55,000 people showed up for Atlanta United FC's first game. Team owner Arthur Blank kept getting texts from Major League Soccer Commissioner Don Garber. He wanted Blank to check the crowd numbers. Before Atlanta's first game in 2017, the best-attended opening weekend match drew only half as many fans.

Blank wasn't surprised. "I love the NFL, and I love the Atlanta Falcons fans. But soccer fans take it to the next level," Blank told a reporter from Channel 11.

Anton Walkes (*left*) reacts as New York Red Bulls midfielder Daniel Royer celebrates scoring a goal on a free kick against Atlanta United.

Dreams of winning their first game ended for the players in the second half. New York's Daniel Royer used his head—and sent the ball flying into the goal. Just six minutes later, the Red Bulls scored again. Worse, the goal was charged to Atlanta player Anton Walkes. After a pass from Kemar Lawrence, New York's Bradley Wright-Phillips sent the ball toward the goal. Instead of stopping it, Walkes kicked it in.

Losing hurt. Still, fans were patient. After all, the city had waited more than 20 years for a Major League Soccer team.

Blank was an experienced sports team owner, as owner of the Falcons. For years he pushed to bring pro soccer to Atlanta as well.In 2008, he approached MLS. League officials turned him down. They didn't think the pro football stadium was right for soccer. At first, Blank couldn't raise money to build a soccer-only stadium.

The place where a soccer team plays is called the home pitch. The first Major League Soccer home pitches sometimes shared them with other sports. Today New York City FC shares Yankee Stadium with the Major League Baseball team. The New England Revolution and the Seattle Sounders play on fields designed for football. One reason for the League's success is that new team fields are best designed for soccer.

In 2013, Blank had enough money to build a new stadium. The Falcons would play there. But he promised it would be designed for *both* types of football. The next year, MLS expanded to Atlanta.

Blank was ready. He'd had a soccer field designed before the city got an MLS team. Atlanta's new Mercedes-Benz Stadium would be the first in the League constructed with both sports in mind.

Players and fans alike prefer a stadium built just for soccer, like Mercedes-Benz Stadium.

Football stadiums aren't great for soccer. The field is narrower. At Atlanta's stadium, seats along the corner of the field can be pushed back. Across MLS, home pitches range from 70–77 yards wide. Atlanta's would be 75. The fields are between 110–120 yards long. Mercedes-Benz Stadium is 115 yards long. Besides being one of the bigger fields for MLS, it was also the right size for future World Cup games.

The other problem with sharing a field is that most MLS teams draw around 21,000 fans. They get swallowed up by huge football stadiums built for crowds three times that size. Atlanta's new stadium would have curtains covering 30,000 upper-deck seats. This way soccer fans could sit together instead of spread out across a huge mostly empty stadium.

It was a big project. Even as the stadium was constructed, training facilities were also planned.

Atlanta United FC's home pitch, Mercedes-Benz Stadium, cost $1.5 billion. It also took longer than planned. For most of the spring and summer, Atlanta United FC's home games were played at Georgia Tech's Bobby Dodd Stadium. By then, the team was used to winning.

Their first away game was against another brand new United expansion team. On March 12, 2017, Atlanta United crushed Minnesota United 6–1. The next week the players returned home and beat Chicago Fire 4–0. The team won more often at home. Fans and players endured the summer heat and a college stadium.

On September 10th, Atlanta United was finally able to play at Mercedes-Benz Stadium. They beat Dallas 3–0. A few days later, their opponent had just as hard a time scoring. Maybe it was the heat. Maybe it was the humidity. Atlanta beat the New England Revolution 7–0.

The September 16th game against Orlando City ended in a draw, but still set a record. More than 70,000 people showed up for the game at Mercedes-Benz Stadium. In the final game of the season on October 22, Atlanta United played before nearly 72,000 fans.

Atlanta's Hector Villalba (*left*) is defended by Orlando City's Dillon Powers during a match in September 2017.

The team's president first played soccer in England. Darren Eales told a *Guardian* reporter, "I look back 23 years ago when I was playing in America, we were lucky to get a thousand people a game and the biggest cheer was when the goalkeeper punted the ball high into the air."

The team was ranked fourth in the Eastern Conference. Atlanta U became the first expansion team in seven years to reach the playoffs the first year. Atlanta didn't reach the playoffs by hiring stars. They hired young, fast players who believed in teamwork and understood the rules of the game.

Fun Facts

1 The team's colors are the same ones as the Falcons used when they began in 1966: Red, black, and gold. For away games, players wear white uniforms with red trim.

2 Since 2004, seven of the 13 expansion teams have had FC or SC in their names. There are two other United teams, in Minnesota and Washington, D.C.

3 At Atlanta United FC's Academy, soccer players aged 12 to 18 are being turned into top athletes. Atlanta United hopes a few will be good enough to join the team.

Winning Style

CHAPTER THREE

Soccer stars are different. In other sports, stars are a big reason why their teams win championships. The team is usually only as good as its star player. In soccer, the team is only as good as its weakest link. It takes many passes to get a goal. If one player makes a mistake, the whole team suffers. Teamwork is important in every sport, but soccer fans believe teamwork is even more important than in sports like football, basketball, and baseball.

It took years before Georgia got a popular pro soccer team. Meanwhile, lots of Georgians weren't watching soccer. They were *playing* it. The need for teamwork and a chance to spend time on the field are some of the reasons lot of kids play soccer. It's also easy to learn but hard to master. That means you can understand the basics right away.

Most sports need special equipment. Soccer can be played at the beach, in a backyard, or a park. All you need is a ball and something for a goal line.

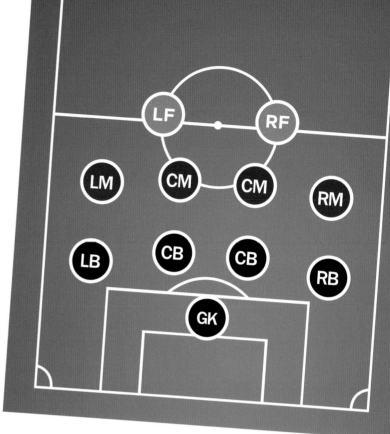

Goalkeeper(GK)
Right back defender (RB)
Left back defender (LB)
Center back defender (CB)
Left midfielder (LM)
Center midfielder (CM)
Right midfielder (RM)
Left forward (LF)
Right forward (RF)

Each side has eleven players. The goalie usually wears a different color so the referee can tell goalkeepers apart from their teammates. Goalies are allowed to use their hands near the goal to keep the ball from going in.

Beside the goalie, the ten other players line up in a 4-4-2 formation. Four players form one line. Four more stand behind them. The final two stay closest to the other team's goal.

The defenders stay closest to their own team's goal. They try to keep the other side from scoring.

Midfielders are called that because they stay around the middle of the field. These four players can attack. They can also defend. Attacking midfielders move the ball toward the other team's goal. Defending midfielders move it away from their team's goal. No matter what they do, they have to keep the ball in play. They usually have the ball more than the other players. This makes it a tough position with a lot of running. The team leader or captain is often the center midfielder.

The final two positions are the forwards. Their job is to drive the ball into their opponent's goal.

Substitute players can be called in from the bench. Each team gets three. If a player is subbed out, he can't go back to the field.

Soccer has two halves. Each half is 45 minutes. Because the clock doesn't stop during pauses in play, the referee adds time at the end of the half.

From school teams to pro teams, away games are hard. Travel is tiring. The field is unfamiliar. The opposing team's hometown crowd is usually louder.

Soccer teams talk about a 12th player. That player is represented by the fans watching the game. Their energy motivates the players. Atlanta United FC even gave those fans their own number—17.

Still, in the first few months of play, Atlanta had as many challenges at home as away. After

Soccer teams like to call their fans the '12th player,' because their cheers are as important as having another player on the field.

four games on the road, the team returned to Atlanta only to lose on April 30th to D.C. United. The next day, team Captain Michael Parkhurst told a reporter from the *Atlanta Journal Constitution*, "We've shown we can get results on the road. We have to. We missed this opportunity today. It's our only home game in a seven-game span and we took nothing from it. We have to pick up points on the road."

In July, the team faced its biggest rival, Orlando City. The team even posted a billboard in its opponent's downtown: "Orlando, we're coming to conquer." Although Atlanta players won their first meeting on July 21, 1 to 0, their next two matches ended in a draw.

Throughout the summer, the team improved at home. The players were working together better. Atlanta United is not just new to Major League Soccer. Many of its players are new as well. "We felt we could get better players, if we got younger players building up their career rather than taking a player halfway on the beach," team President Darren Eales told *Fast Company* magazine.

These players are fast and aggressive. Atlanta often has higher scoring games. Instead of getting one or two goals, Atlanta often gets six, even seven. The team focuses on offense. This means players put a lot of energy into driving across the field and scoring.

Many of Atlanta United's players have just begun playing as professionals. Some planned to move on to European teams. But with a winning record, many have decided to stay.

Fun Facts

1 Atlanta United's motto is "Unite and Conquer." Pictures with the word "Conquer" show the soccer players. Pictures with the word "Unite" show off fans.

2 The team logo is a circle with an A in the middle. Behind it are five red and black stripes. Some call the team "The Five Stripes."

The United's Best

Gerardo "Tata" Martino had played and coached all over the world. As Atlanta United FC's new coach, he worked hard to find players who could succeed. He demanded a fast, aggressive style. Many of the players who joined the team did so because of the coach.

Martino knew he was competing for players with teams from all over the world. Yet many of the younger players would have had more time on the bench and less time on the field with better-known teams in Europe.

Atlanta United's players haven't had as long to prove themselves as the ones at other teams. They have only played in Atlanta for one or two seasons. Still, a few set themselves apart.

Here are some of the top players from 2017–2018:

Miguel Almirón

Miguel Almirón
Midfielder (2017-2018)

The star player from Paraguay, Almirón's pro career began when he was 14 years old. To get Almirón, Atlanta United paid an $8 million transfer fee to his former team, Argentina's Club Atlético Lanús. Almirón was a big part of Atlanta United's winning strategy and is often called the team's heartbeat. On May 20th, he scored the team's second hat trick—getting three goals in a single game. He also played in the 2017 MLS All Star team.

George Bello
Defender (2018)

Born in Nigeria, Bello's family moved to Georgia when he was young. Signed to Atlanta United when he was 16 years old, he is on the roster for both United and its reserve team, Atlanta United 2.

Chapter Four

Andrew Carleton
Winger (2017, 2018)

In 2016, Carleton began playing with United Soccer League's Charleston Battery. He became the youngest pro player to start a USL match. He played in a preseason game against Chattanooga FC in 2017 and made his regular season debut as a substitute player on May 20, 2017. In 2018, he played for both Atlanta United and the reserve team, Atlanta United 2.

Josef Martínez
Center Forward, Striker (2017–2018)

Beginning as a professional in Venezuela, Martinez scored a hat trick (three goals) in Atlanta United's second game. Despite a series of injuries, he reached five hat tricks faster than any player in MLS history. In March 2017, he was named MLS Player of the Month. By summer 2018, he had scored more than 40 goals for Atlanta.

Josef Martínez

Michael Parkhurst
Team Captain, Defender (2017-2018)

Growing up in Providence, Rhode Island, Parkhurst began his career with the region's MLS team, the New England Revolution. He was named MLS Rookie of the Year in 2005 and Defender of the Year two years later. After several years overseas beginning in 2008, he returned to MLS in 2014. In late 2016 he was traded to Atlanta from Columbus Crew SC. He has played on the MLS All Star team five times, including while with Atlanta in 2017.

Greg Garza
Left Back (2017, 2018)

Born in Grapevine, Texas, Garza got his pro start with Mexico's Primera División reserve team Club Tijuana in 2011. Signed to Atlanta United FC in December of 2016 for a one-year loan, he was given a multi-year contract by the end of the first season. He also played on the MLS All Star team in 2017.

Fun Facts

1 Several of the teenage Homegrown Players who began on the reserve team have also played for Atlanta United.

2 In 1912, Juliette Gordon Low founded the Girl Scouts of America in Savannah, Georgia. Ninety-nine years later, teen-ager Emily Rose earned the highest Girl Scout honors, the Gold Award, for a soccer manual she created for a team of 10-year-old girls.

Communicating in Atlanta

Atlanta United players didn't want to wait. They wanted to win.

Team owner Arthur Blank realized that most expansion teams spend years developing players. Those teams often spend the time near last place in the rankings. Atlanta's team would be different.

The team's first year, Atlanta reached the playoffs. Their strategy was to **recruit** from other countries. Every MLS team can select up to eight **international** players. Team Director Carlos Bocanegra believed he would need every one of them. He had played pro soccer in France, England, Scotland, and Spain. In July 2015 he told a reporter, "We're not trying to be a foreign team. It's going to be very tough to get all of our talent from here in America right from the get-go."

Atlanta United FC midfielder Kevin Kratz (*right*) is challenged by Miami FC midfielder Dylan Mares.

In its first two seasons, Atlanta's lineup included Jon Gallagher from Ireland, Miguel Almirón from Paraguay, and Kevin Kratz from Germany. They shared the field with hometown heroes from Georgia like Alec Kann, Andrew Carleton, and 16-year-old George Bello. Players arrived in Atlanta from Europe, South America, and Africa. Many of the players spoke different languages. They had different backgrounds. And they all had to communicate.

To Blank, the first step was making sure the players got along with each other, both on and off the field. To help them bond, the team hosts karaoke nights. The newest player has to sing first.

Chapter Five

Atlanta United midfielder Chris McCann, (*left*), is collared by Seattle Sounders defender Kim Kee-Hee during a game in July 2018.

Lots of MLS teams have international players. The difference is, Atlanta has *young* international players. "People were saying, 'You're going out there, you're going to play in a league that everyone goes to when they're finishing their career,'" Midfielder Chris McCann told a reporter from *The Irish Times*. "But when you come and actually try it for yourself, you realize it's not actually like that at all." Instead the 31-year-old was joined on the team by a fellow Irishman, 22-year-old forward Jon Gallagher. Beyond the European players, McCann noticed something, telling a reporter, "There's a lot of good South American players here, which people probably don't realize or have never heard of back in (England)."

Those South American players often arrived speaking little English. They would use Spanish terms like *el equipo* for the team, *el capitán* for the team captain and *el director técnico* for the coach. Spanish-speaking soccer players aren't rare. What is unusual is that Atlanta's "el director técnico"—Head Coach Tata Martino—arrived in Atlanta speaking little English. Team Communications Coordinator Justin Veldhuis often translates for Martino and the other players.

Veldhuis grew up speaking English but learned Spanish in school and in Madrid, Spain. The hard part is, he told writer Haris Kruskic, "Every country speaks a different brand of Spanish. The coaches and players have different ways of saying things and a different slang, and it's all a little different Spanish than what I learned in Madrid."

Martino speaks a formal Spanish, the kind taught in school. He also will speak nonstop for several minutes, while Miguel Almirón takes his time. Besides Veldhuis, the players all work hard to communicate and understand what the coach wants.

Their hard work paid off. By the start of the 2018 season, the team was ranked No. 1 in the League. After losing their first game, teammembers returned home to beat D.C. United in front of 72,000 fans. They wouldn't lose again until their tenth game of the season, in May. Then in December they became victorious by winning the MLS Cup. Atlanta United players defeated Portland by 2-0 before a record-size crowd of 73,019. They had won the prize in only their second season in the major leagues.

Eales told *Inc.* magazine that one thing was even more important than winning games: The fans. "The moment we start to take our fans for granted is the moment that this is going to disappear." In just two years, Atlanta United has proven that soccer can succeed in the South. They've done it with a fast paced game and fans who won't give up.

Fun Fact

In 2018, Atlanta United filled its international roster with three players from Argentina and one player each from Ireland, Germany, and Paraguay.

What You Should Know

- Modern soccer began in England around 1830.

- The name soccer came from England.

- The United States, Canada, Japan, and Korea are among the few countries that do not call the game football.

- Atlanta United became the first expansion team in seven years to reach the playoffs its first year.

- Early MLS team names were like ones in other U.S. sports. They were nouns—like the L.A. Galaxy, the Dallas Burn. Today the team is FC Dallas. Like many other teams in MLS, it reminds fans of European teams like Manchester United.

- Atlanta Head Coach Head Coach Gerardo "Tata" Martino is a native Spanish speaker who is learning English.

- Atlanta United FC shares a new stadium with pro football team, the Atlanta Falcons. The stadium cost $1.5 billion.

- It took nearly ten years for Atlanta Falcons owner Arthur Blank to get a MLS team in Atlanta.

- Blank started the Home Depot home improvement chain stores.

- There are four main fan organizations: Terminus Legion, Resurgence, the Faction and the Footie Mob. Footie Mob honors the city's hip-hop history with its play on the group Goodie Mob.

- When the U.S, Canada, and Mexico co-host the World Cup in 2026, some games may be played at Atlanta United's stadium.

Quick Stats

2017 First expansion team to reach the playoffs in its first year since 2009.

2018 At the Atlanta Sports Awards, Coach of the Year went to Gerardo "Tata" Martino, Professional Athlete of the Year was Miguel Almirón and Atlanta United won Team of the Year.

1847 Founding of Atlanta, Georgia's largest city.

1906 Future business mogul John H. Harland emigrates to the U.S. from Ireland, bringing his love for soccer with him.

1912 Amateur soccer matches are first played in Atlanta at the city's Piedmont Park.

1920s Employees of the John H. Harland Company form a soccer league.

1958 At Emory University, the state's first college-level soccer play begins. Most of the coaches in the athletic department have to learn how to play.

1966 Moving to Atlanta from Milwaukee, Major League Baseball team the Braves buys the Chiefs, a pro soccer team.

1967 The Atlanta Chiefs begin their first season in North American Soccer League.

1968 The Chiefs team wins the NASL Championship.

1972 The Chiefs team folds.

1979 Millionaire businessman Ted Turner resurrects the Chiefs.

1981 The new Chiefs team folds just like the old team.

2009 Blank, owner of the Atlanta Falcons, requests a MLS team.

2014 Blank is awarded an MLS team.

2017 Atlanta United FC players reach the playoffs their first year. They also set MLS attendance records.

2018 Atlanta United FC sits atop the Eastern Conference.

Glossary

emigrate
Leaving your country to live in another one

immigrant
Person who comes from a different country to live in a new one

international
Players who come from other countries

professional
Performing a job for money

recruiting
Getting someone to play for your team

stadium
A large arena for sports like soccer

tournament
A competition with contests between many teams until one team is the final winner

Further Reading

Crisfield, Deborah. *The Everything Kids Soccer Book*. Simon and Schuster. 2013.

Lock, Deborah. *Soccer School*. DK Publishing. 2015.

Woods, Mark. *Goal! Soccer Facts and Stats*. Gareth Stevens. 2011.

On the Internet

Atlanta United FC Players
https://www.atlutd.com/players

Beginners Guide to Soccer. U.S. National Soccer Team Players.
https://ussoccerplayers.com/beginners-guide-to-soccer

Soccer Positions
ducksters.com, http://www.ducksters.com/sports/soccer/positions.php

Index

About the Author

During my time in Portland, Oregon, I knew when the Timbers had a home game. When fans gathered they would create a parade. The party would spill out into the streets. Everywhere members of the Timbers Army chanted and cheered. In 2014, the World Cup motivated some restaurants to set up tables and giant TV screens in parking lots. Fans arrived sporting the colors of just about every team that qualified. This what I love about soccer. It's what I love about all sports. For me the most interesting part of a game is how fans and teams relate to one another. The way fans are honored, even celebrated in soccer seems to be unique in sports. The way Atlanta soccer fans responded to keep their sport and their teams going makes a great story. I loved writing about Atlanta United and the brand new team's enthusiastic fans who have broken attendance records. **—John Bankston**